ABC of Hinduism for Kids

ABCD
EFGHIJ
K
X O
LM
NPQR
STUV
WYZ

ॐ

ABC of HINDUISM for KIDS

DEVDUTT PATTANAIK

Illustrated by the author

Illuminated with colour by Debasish Sarma

ALEPH

ALEPH BOOK COMPANY
An independent publishing firm
promoted by ***Rupa Publications India***

First published in India in 2024
by Aleph Book Company
7/16 Ansari Road, Daryaganj
New Delhi 110 002

ISBN: 978-81-19635-74-0

1 3 5 7 9 10 8 6 4 2

Design and typeset by Special Effects Graphics Design Co, Mumbai
Printed in India

Within infinite myths lies an eternal truth
Who sees it all?
Varuna has a thousand eyes
Indra, a hundred
You and I, only two.

Introduction

Over 2,500 years ago, the king of Persia ruled a vast kingdom. The eastern border of his kingdom was marked by a great river.

From beyond that river came the elephants for his army. Those who brought the elephants referred to the eastern river as Sindhu.

'Hindush' in the cuneiform script of the Persians

The king of Persia could not pronounce S, so he referred to the river as Hindu. And he referred to those who lived by this river, and beyond, in the east, as the Hindus.

Later, the Greeks would call this river Indus and the people, who tamed and rode elephants, as Indians, residents of India.

The world of the Hindus was very different from the world of the king of Persia. The king of Persia believed that humans live only once. That they must live this life the right way. And the right way comes from one God, the true God, his God. But the Hindus believed that humans live many lives, that there are many ways to live those many lives, and that gods and goddesses do not tell you how to live—they just help you live these lives and find happiness and maybe even freedom. It was the Hindu way. Some people refer to it as Sanatan Dharma or the forever way of living.

'Hindush' in the hieroglyphic script of the Egyptians

This book will present to you the ABC of that Hindu way, now known as Hinduism to most people around the world.

Just as the king of Persia could not pronounce S, and referred to Sindhu as Hindu, the Hindus did not make words that start with F, W, Q, X, and Z. Different people in the world not only think differently and live differently, but they also speak differently.

atma

Every day the sun rises and sets. Every year the rains come and go. Nothing lasts forever. Plants wither away. Animals get eaten. Humans die. Hindus believe that only the body dies. The atma within the body simply leaves the old body

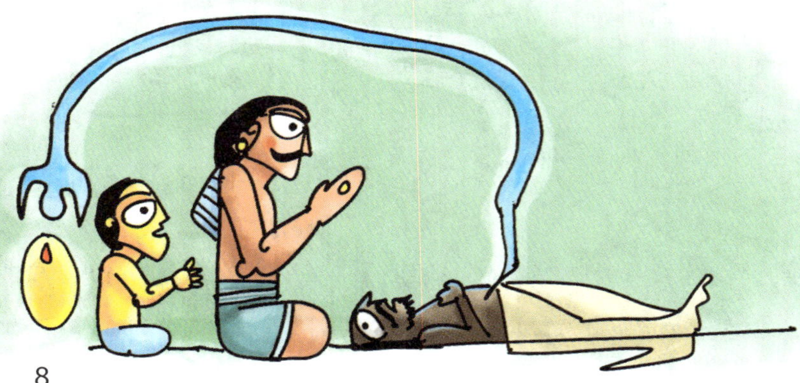

and occupies a new body, like discarding an old garment and wearing a new garment. The atma is resident in the body, unafraid of death, always at peace. The body, however, needs food and protection. Those who are not in touch with the atma, are forever hungry and insecure, so are eternally unhappy. They keep chasing food, are never satisfied, and trapped in unhappy lives.

Brahma

Brahma is the creator. He created life, and so hunger. Hunger makes plants grow, animals move, humans work. Hunger makes us chase food, grab food, hoard food, and fight over food. Hunger is the source of all problems. Hence, no one worships Brahma.

From his four heads came the four Vedas:

- Rig, the Veda of poetry.
- Sama, the Veda of music.
- Yajur, the Veda of rituals.
- Atharva, the Veda of spells.

The Vedas contain knowledge to overcome hunger and be happy. To make this knowledge easier to understand, stories such as the Ramayana, the Mahabharata, the Bhagavata, and the Puranas came into being. Together these stories are called the Fifth Veda.

caste

Every Hindu belongs to a caste, or jati. Originally, members of a jati followed the same profession. A potter's son could only be a potter. Those who belonged to a jati could only marry within it.

Hundreds of jatis were grouped into four categories or varnas:

- Brahmins had access to the Vedas.
- Kshatriyas controlled the land.
- Vaishyas were traders.
- Shudras provided service.

However, over time, some jobs were considered better than others, deserving more money and respect. Other jobs were seen as dirty and polluted. Members of these jatis were told to stay outside the village, not allowed to use the village well, and called 'untouchable'. Today, by law, all Indians can do whatever job they choose and marry who they want. But many people are too afraid to give up these old, even cruel, caste rules.

Devi

Devi means Goddess. Hindus worship both God and Goddess. God created hunger, which no one can see. The Goddess created food that everyone can see. What came first? Hunger or food? God or Goddess? The Goddess takes three forms to match the three forms of God. With Brahma, creator of all hungry and unhappy beings, she is Saraswati, the goddess of knowledge and art, dressed in white, riding a goose, veena in hand. With Vishnu, who gets the hungry to care for each other, she is Lakshmi, the goddess of fortune, dressed in red, surrounded by elephants in a lotus pond, holding a pot overflowing with grain and gold. With Shiva, who destroys hunger, she is Gauri, who tells Shiva to have compassion for those unable to overcome hunger. When he ignores her, she turns into Kali and dances on his chest. When he appreciates her, she turns into Annapurna, who feeds, and Durga, who protects.

elephant

For hundreds of years, India exported elephants and imported horses. Elephants can uproot trees, break rocks, and forge a path where there never was one. With elephants, kings could build highways through dense forests and over steep mountains. Elephants live in lands with a lot of plants. Where there are a lot of plants there is a lot of rain, a lot of water, and a lot of food. Thus elephants represent power and wealth, closely linked to Lakshmi, the goddess of fortune, and much loved by Indra, the king of the devas. Elephant-headed Ganesha removes all barriers, all obstacles. That is why Hindus chant Ganesha's name before starting any activity. He brings good luck, prosperity, and peace.

forest

In the forest, the big eats the small. All those who eat eventually get eaten. No one helps anyone. There are no rules, no right or wrong. This is matsya-nyaya, or fish-justice, the way of the forest, suitable for plants and animals, but not humans. Humans tame forests, create fields

and gardens, and establish culture. Dharma is a culture where the strong help the weak. Adharma is a culture where the strong exploit the weak. The Ramayana and Mahabharata tell stories where kings such as Ram and the Pandavas are forced to live in the forest, to learn the value of kings and rules and dharma.

G

Ganga

Ganga is the river goddess who rides a dolphin and holds a pot. Once she flowed in the sky, with the devas. Devas are immortal; they cannot die. Humans, who live on earth, are mortal; they die. To help humans overcome death, and get another chance of life, the gods told Ganga to go to earth. Her fall from the sky would have cracked the earth. But Shiva caught her midway in the thick locks of his hair. She then flowed gently down the mountains towards the sea. When Hindus die, the body is burnt, and the ashes are thrown into the Ganga. Ganga helps the dead be reborn. Hindus also bathe in the Ganga to clean body and mind, and start afresh.

Hanuman

Hindus worship Hanuman, a wise and mighty monkey, who stands in temples with a tree in one hand, a mountain in the other, crushing a demon under his feet. Son of the wind god Vayu, student of the sun god Surya, he was extremely strong and clever—a warrior, a diplomat, a scholar, and an artist. Thanks to his understanding of the Vedas, he was content with life. But he used his immense strength and

knowledge to help others. He protected the monkey-king, Sugriva, from his violent elder brother, Vali. He helped Ram rescue his wife, Sita, from the clutches of the rakshasa-king, Ravana. In exchange, he asked for nothing except more opportunities to serve those in need.

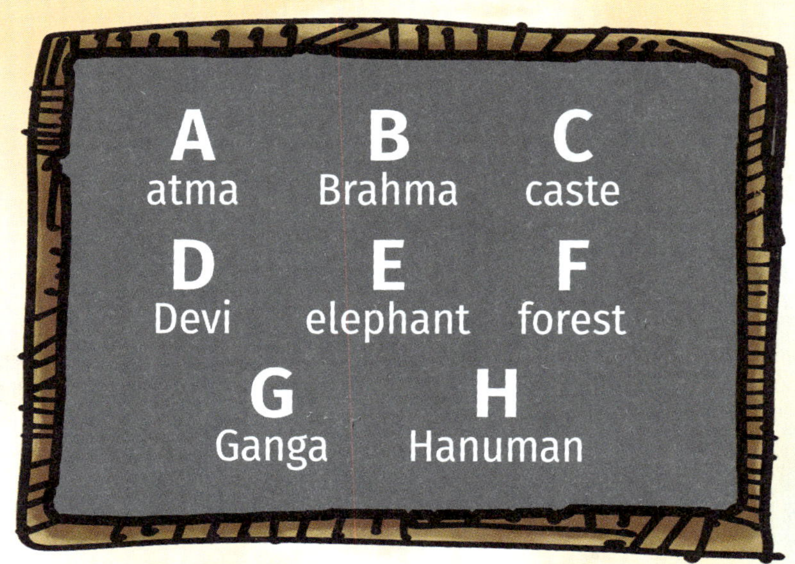

What will the other words be?

I J K
L M N
O P Q
R S T
U V W
X Y Z

Indra

Indra is king of the devas. The devas live in the sky, in Swarga, where there is the wish-fulfilling tree, Kalpataru, the wish-fulfilling cow, Kamadhenu, the wish-fulfilling jewel, Chintamani, and the nectar of immortality, Amrit. The asuras who live under the earth, in Patala, keep attacking Swarga, and demanding a portion of what the devas have. For

asuras and devas are half-brothers, sons of the same father, Brahma, by different mothers. The devas refuse to share. They defeat the asuras with the help of Shiva, Vishnu, or Devi. But the asuras always return. Because the asuras have Sanjivani Vidya, a secret by which the dead can be regenerated. As a result, Indra's Swarga has prosperity, without peace.

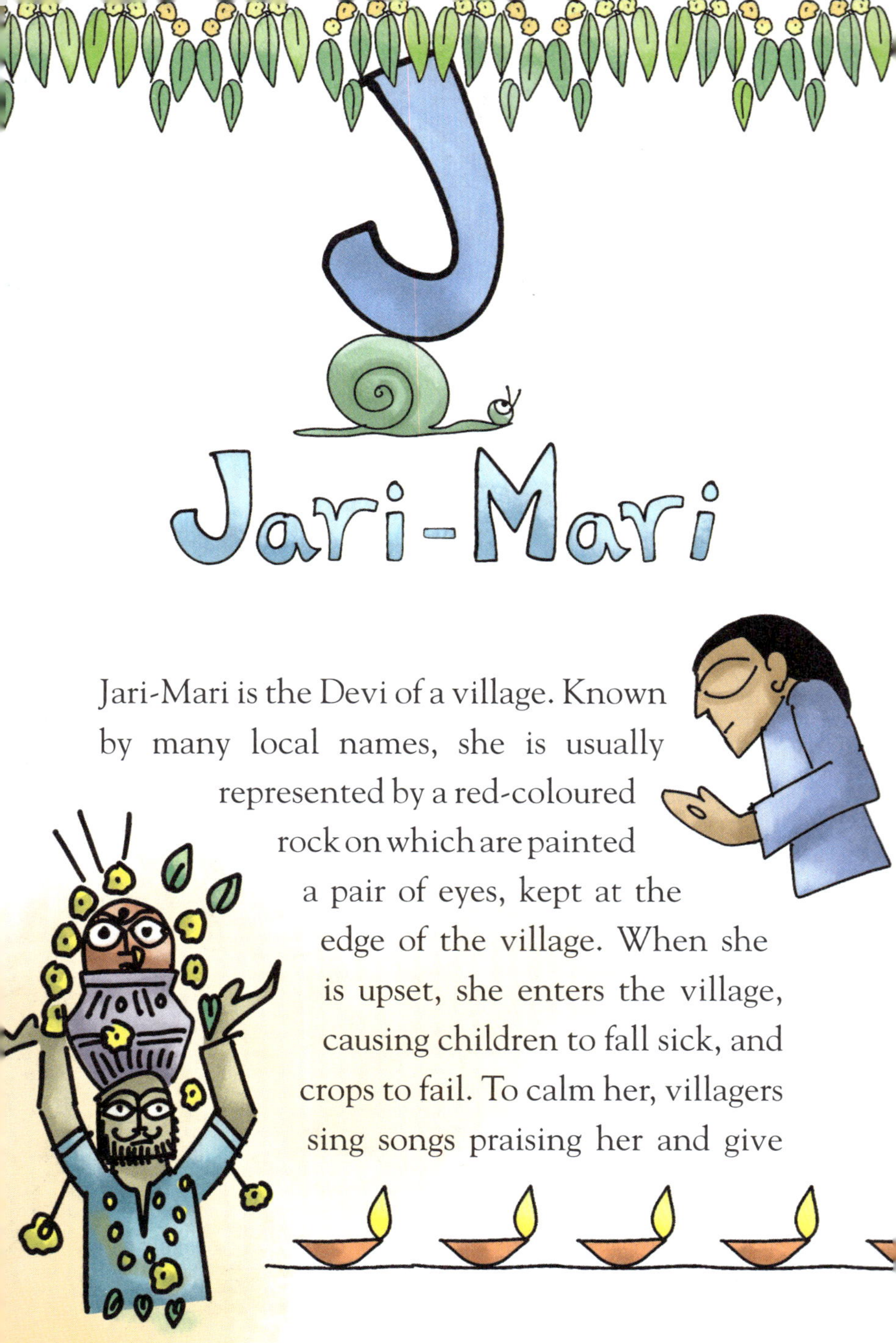

J

Jari-Mari

Jari-Mari is the Devi of a village. Known by many local names, she is usually represented by a red-coloured rock on which are painted a pair of eyes, kept at the edge of the village. When she is upset, she enters the village, causing children to fall sick, and crops to fail. To calm her, villagers sing songs praising her and give her food she likes—sour lemons, bitter neem, hot spicy chillies. Her companions are offered meat and alcohol. People whip themselves, walk on fire, and torture their bodies for the crimes the village may have committed unknowingly. Pleased, Jari-Mari leaves the village. Then the healing begins. Fevers go away. Rain falls. Health returns. Jari-Mari is a folk way of remembering the pain and suffering of plants and animals destroyed to make a village.

Kama is the god of pleasure. He rides a parrot, holds a sugarcane bow, and has a bowstring made of bees and butterflies. When he shoots his arrows of flowers, the mind is filled with a craving for pleasure. He brings joy and takes away boredom. But he is also addictive. He makes people forget all responsibilities. Irritated by Kama's temptations,

Shiva opened his third eye, located on his forehead, released a missile of fire, which set Kama afire and reduced him to ashes. But Vishnu and Devi brought Kama back to life as life without fun is no life at all.

leela

Leela means play-acting to benefit others. Hindu gods love to do leela. They want nothing from humans, but they pretend to be needy to check if humans are generous and sincere. For example, in the Bhagavata, Krishna, who is Vishnu on earth, plays games with his mother and with milkmaids, stealing their butter and their clothes,

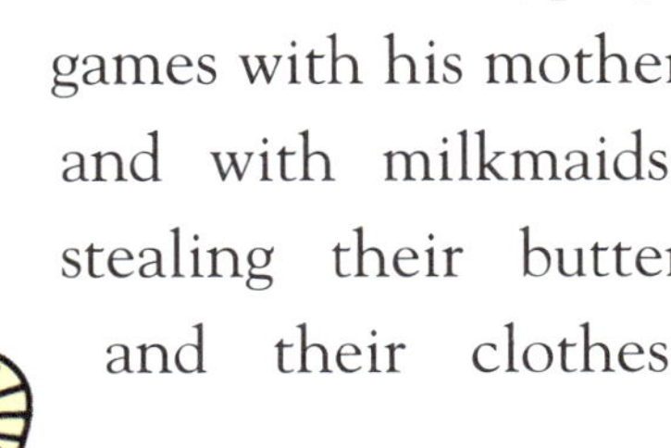

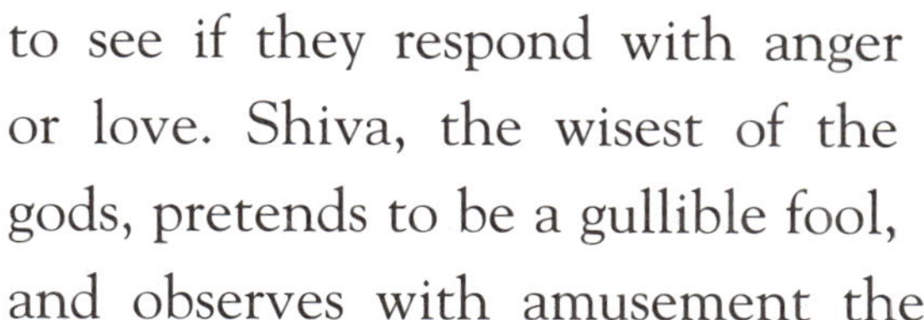

to see if they respond with anger or love. Shiva, the wisest of the gods, pretends to be a gullible fool, and observes with amusement the insatiable greed of those who pray to him.

The gods know that those who take, but do not give, are trapped forever in the wheel of birth and death.

mandir

Mandir means a temple, a home of a Hindu god. Here images of gods are housed permanently. They are bathed, adorned, admired, fed, and entertained with music, song, and dance. The gods even go on chariot rides and boat rides on special festival days. The temples have a pyramidal roof to remind the world about Mount Meru, the sacred mountain in the centre of the world, from which flow all the rivers that nourish the earth. In front of the temple is a hall for devotees. People gather here to meet the gods, greet them, praise them, make offerings, and then seek solutions to their problems.

Nataraja

Nataraja means the dancing Shiva. At first, Shiva did not dance. He sat still with his eyes shut. His body was covered with ash. Serpents slithered on his body. He was content by himself, uninterested in life. What about those around you, said the Goddess. They are unhappy and miserable. Reveal to them the

secret of contentment. Make life interesting for them. So, Shiva began to dance. He moved his hands, legs, hips, head, eyes, fingers, and lips in rhythm. But this was no ordinary dance. Shiva was communicating the rhythm of the universe—the unending cycle of creation and destruction.

Om

Om is the most ancient and most holy Hindu sound. It is like ringing the doorbell to enter the house of the gods. Hindus use many different sounds to connect with the universe. These sounds are called mantras. When the sounds have no meaning, they are called bija-mantra, or seed-sounds. Om is the

most important bija-mantra. Japa-mantra is when the sound captures the name of a god, such as Ram, Krishna, or Shiva. The sound can also contain an action. For example, Om Namo Shiva is an action mantra, saluting Shiva. Om Namo Narayana is an action mantra saluting Vishnu.

P

Puja

Puja means worship. It is conducted privately inside homes, and publicly in temples. Images of gods are placed on a special seat. The gods are invited to occupy these images. They are welcomed with lamps and bells, and incense,

bathed with milk and scented water, adorned with garments, ornaments, and flowers, fed their favourite food, praised in songs, entertained with music and dance. It is hoped that happy gods will ensure health, happiness, peace, and prosperity all around. This is the ritual of exchange—where you give in order to receive. As per the Vedas, this is how you establish relationships and create civilization.

A
atma
B
Brahma
C
caste
D
Devi
E
elephant
F
forest
G
Ganga
H
Hanuman
I
Indra
J
Jari-Mari
K
Kama
L
leela
M
mandir
N
Nataraja
O
Om
P
puja

What will the other words be?
Q R S
T U V
W X
Y Z

quarter

If we divide something into four parts, then we get four quarters. In Hinduism, we find many things divided into four parts.

Human existence has four goals:

1. Dharma, responsibility.
2. Artha, success.
3. Kama, fun.
4. Moksha, spirituality.

The cycle of life has four phases or ashrams:

1. Brahmacharya, when we are students.
2. Grihastha, when we have families.
3. Vanaprastha, when we retire from work.
4. Sanyasa, when we give up everything.

Rakshasa

Hinduism has no word for evil. But there are demons, monsters, troublemakers, who spread unhappiness and so are trapped in the wheel of rebirth. There are rakshasas in the forest who grab and take whatever they want. There is Kabandha of the Ramayana whose head and stomach are one, and who grabs humans with his long arms. There is Baka of the Mahabharata who attacks villages, eats all the food, and then eats the villagers too.

There are asuras who live under the earth who constantly attack the paradise of the gods and do not let them live in peace. There are pretas and bhutas and pisachas who are ghosts who torment the living, as they are unable to cross the river Vaitarni and enter the land of the dead.

Major events in a Hindu's life are marked by a ceremony. These are called samskara. Such ceremonies remind humans they are not animals. These rituals include:

1. The first shaving of the baby's head.
2. The first time the baby eats solid food.
3. The first piercing of the ear to wear earrings.
4. The start of education.
5. The end of education.
6. Marriage
7. Childbirth
8. Death

In Hinduism, time or kala is worshipped. Time ensures all things that start have a finish, and all things that finish eventually restart. So summer and winter follow each other. Day and night follow

each other. War and peace follow each other. Life and death follow each other. The Hindu world, therefore, is eternal, without beginning and end. Hindus believe that the human lifespan is equal to the blink of an eye of Indra. Indra's lifespan is equal to Brahma's blink. Brahma's lifespan is equal to Vishnu's blink. Vishnu's lifespan is equal to Shiva's blink. The world ends when Vishnu sleeps and begins when he awakens.

Hindus love festivals or utsav. There are festivals in spring, summer, autumn, and winter. There are festivals before the rain, during the rain and after the rain, festivals when the moon is waxing, and the moon is waning. There are festivals to celebrate the birth of Ram and Krishna; festivals to celebrate the marriage of Shiva; festivals to celebrate the killing of demons; a festival of colours like Holi;

a festival of lamps like Diwali; festivals to celebrate poets; festivals to celebrate the harvest; festivals for women; festivals for brothers and sisters. Festivals are a time to remember the gods, buy new clothes, eat tasty food, visit friends and temples, and enjoy all the wonderful things about life, while being grateful as well as generous.

Vishnu

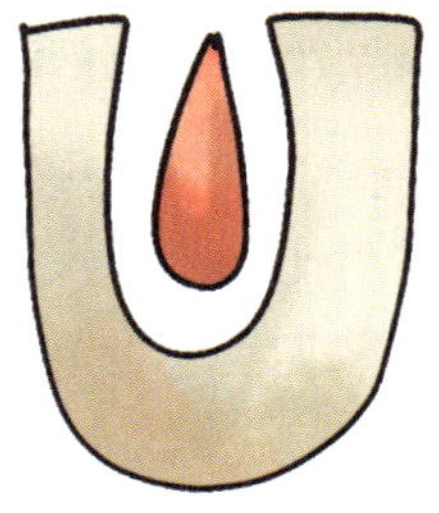

Vishnu sleeps on the coils of a serpent on an ocean of milk called Vaikuntha and rides an eagle called Garuda. He has four hands in which he holds the conch-shell, the wheel, the mace, and the lotus. He is dressed in silks, perfumes, pearls, and flowers. He is a delightful and charming god, teaching everyone about dharma. From time to time

Vishnu takes avatars—he descends on earth and lives like a mortal to show people how to be content and still work to satisfy other people's hungers. Famous avatars include Ram, the king, and Krishna, the cowherd. Vishnu knows that hunger and insecurity make people cunning and devious. He outsmarts the oversmart with a smile. This is why Lakshmi, the goddess of fortune, adores him.

war

The Hindus wrote many stories such as the Ramayana and Mahabharata to understand war and peace. War, said the sages, happens when we focus only on our hunger and ignore other people's hunger. Hunger makes us grab and hoard food. Often war is fought to establish dharma—to force people to share, reclaim what has been stolen, repay what they owe. When we fight for dharma, we do not hate the enemy. In fact, in dharma, there is no villain—just people who are too scared, and too hungry, to be nice. To avoid war, we must exchange—give in order to get. This is the principle behind Hindu rituals such as yagna and puja.

10

How do you write the number 10? The ancient Romans wrote it as X. But ancient Indians wrote it as 10, the numeral one followed by a zero. If you add another zero, you get 100, spelt as hundred, written as C

by the Romans. If you add still another zero, you get 1000, spelt as thousand, written as M by the Romans. So one thousand one hundred and ten was written as MCX in ancient Rome, and as 1110 in ancient India. The Indian way of writing numbers was taken by Arabs to Europe. Hinduism is not just about gods and goddesses, it is also about giving birth to ideas that can be shared with the world.

Yama

Yama is the Hindu god of death. He rides a buffalo. With his noose, he pulls out the preta from within the living body. That is when death happens. The preta becomes a pitr, an ancestor,

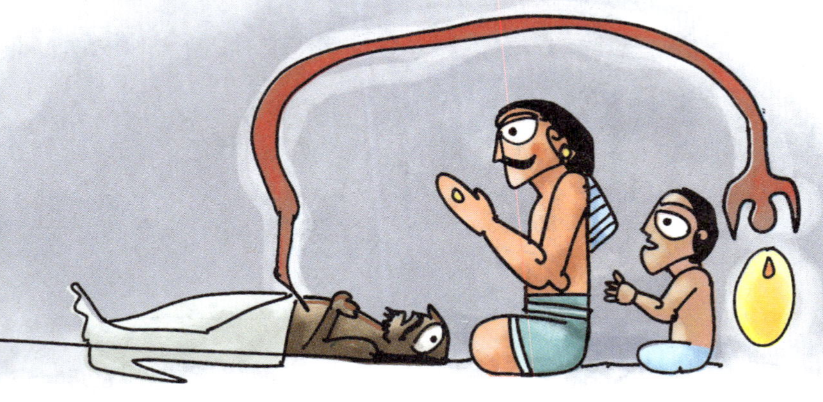

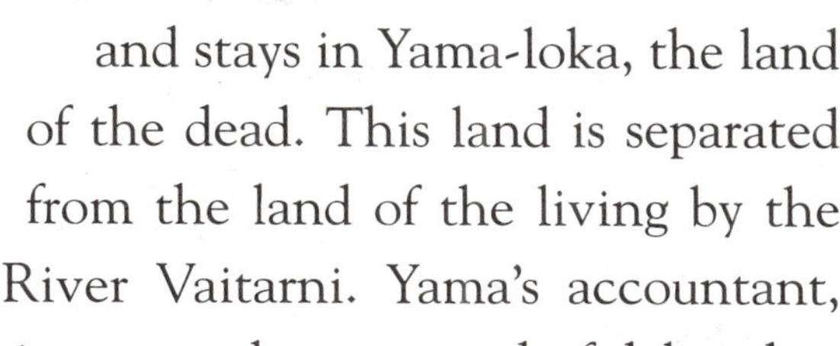

and stays in Yama-loka, the land of the dead. This land is separated from the land of the living by the River Vaitarni. Yama's accountant, Chitragupta, has a record of debts that every pitr owes the world. As long as there are debts to repay, the pitr is bound to be reborn. This is the law of karma. Yama decides the time and place of rebirth based on the debts. When there are no more debts, there is no more rebirth. There is freedom, or moksha.

Zebu

Hindus worship cows. But not all cows, only cows with a hump—the zebu. In cows, the hump represents Mount Meru, the mountain in the centre of the world, from where spring all rivers. The zebu represents Gomata, mother earth. Plants, that nourish all life, are her milk. Vishnu is her cowherd, hence known as Gopala. He descends on earth as Krishna to protect the earth from human greed. Krishna's heaven is called Goloka, the abode of cows. Vishnu's heaven is the ocean of milk, where there is plenty of food for all.

Such a world is possible when everyone is content like Shiva. In temples, Shiva is worshipped as a free-standing rock, the Shiva linga. The zebu bull is referred to as Shiva's bull or Nandi because the hump on its back reminds Hindus of a Shiva linga.

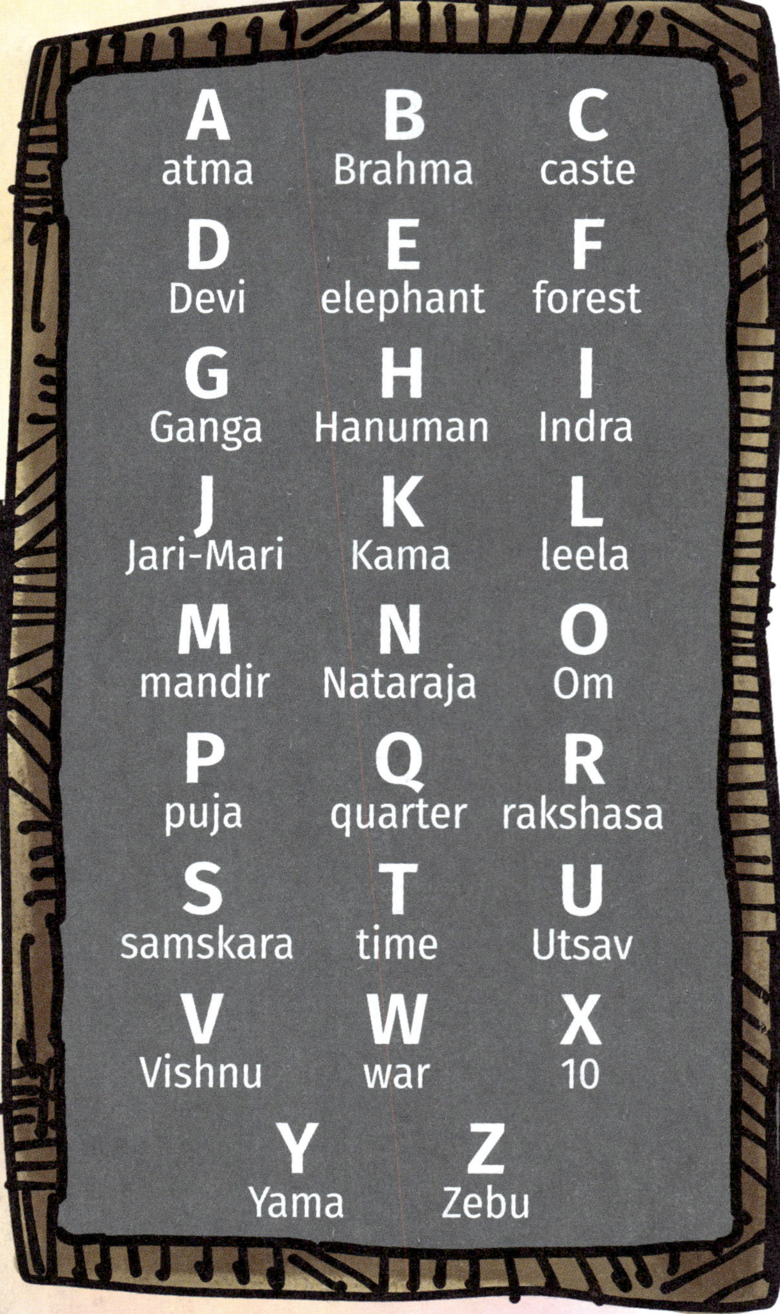
A
atma
B
Brahma
C
caste
D
Devi
E
elephant
F
forest
G
Ganga
H
Hanuman
I
Indra
J
Jari-Mari
K
Kama
L
leela
M
mandir
N
Nataraja
O
Om
P
puja
Q
quarter
R
rakshasa
S
samskara
T
time
U
Utsav
V
Vishnu
W
war
X
10
Y
Yama
Z
Zebu

How many ideas do you remember now?